I0842610

A Paper World

A. Barns-Collier

© Copyright 2021, All Rights Reserved

Summary

It is often said that people are defined by what is written on paper; at least, what is written about them. Whether a military commander decides on promoting a subordinate, or a CEO looking through resumes for a position, what is written on paper determines the individual's fate. A person, in general, is taught to sell themselves to an employer; just like the proverbial deal with the devil, when a person sells their soul. This is not to say that working for an employer is evil, and all employers are the devil, rather that we have been taught a way to live our lives that is based on paper. Whether in a business, in a movie script, or a news article, we live our lives, and base our decisions, off of information that was written on paper. We live in a world of paper. In fact, as trees can be a source of paper, we are surrounding by it.

A resume was originally written on paper, textbooks were written on paper, and business reports were written on paper. However, while much of this appeared to change in the digital age, the same practice prevailed. This is, impart, due to the control measures that were put in place. Therefore, when looking at these objects in the digital space, we still look at two dimensional figures that are based on paper. Rather than basing our actions around physical and hands-on experience, we base our decisions by what has been written, and what we have read. This is, impart, because work based on one's hand is considered abhorrent; a skilled trade craft. On the other hand, what is written does not always translate to reality. A lack of physical experience can be a great downside, when it comes to completing any task. Therefore, many businesses include interviews, as part of their hiring process. Unfortunately, due to resumes and cover letters, hiring managers will often bring preconceived notions to the interview, and have already decided on a candidate, beforehand. In some ways, you could say that the paper world is a figment of the past, but, in other ways, we never really left it.

Dangerous Subjects

Taking an alternative approach, the Orchid Trail is a series of trade stations, set-up along the American land bridge; which is often referred to as Mexico and Central America. Through the use of reason and patterns, it is clear that trade existed between the American hemispheres, but something destroyed this ancient society. The most common cause for such an occurrence is war, but other possibilities can be found. While it is probable that war weakened the ancient civilization of the Americas, an invading culture could have pushed the old inhabitants out of North America. There is a clear difference between South American and North American design. Furthermore, other contrasts exist between the earlier peoples of North America and South America. Very few groups in the North American region practiced a sedentary lifestyle, and those that did were not well considered by other groups. Conversely, from the Aztec of Mexico to the Guaraní and Quechua, sedentary culture is the most prevalent in South America. Sure, some groups hunt, but there is a clear lack of nomadic influence south of the Mexico-U.S. border.

Now, two solidifying features exist that prove well established trade between the two hemispheres. First, the similarity in constructed buildings shows a trade route, while the second reason can be found in particular dog breeds. It is reported that the Aztec, Mayan, and Inca traveled with large packs of dogs; which appeared almost wild, when compared to the house pets of today. The xoloitzcuintli dog breed bares an obvious relation to the Peruvian Inca Orchid. Thus, the name Orchid Trail is very apt for our ancient trade route. Now, let us imagine for a moment that these old cultures built major pyramids in the north. What are often referred to as mounds, are all that remains of these great pyramids, or possible cities. Additionally, the great city of Chaco was likely a part of this ancient trading causeway. Drifting away from the first peoples, we come to the current indigenous peoples of North America, and we see a striking contrast between them and the Aztec. Whether it be the Comanche of the South-West or the Osage further east, the cultures of North America are heavily based in nomadic customs. Therefore, to say that the peoples of North America built the mounds therein, is to say that the nomadic Numidians built Petra; which is an illogical and irrational argument. Some would have us believe that our eyes betray us, and all of the similarities, or contradictions, that exist in this part of the world are simply coincidence. Furthermore, these same individuals would tell us that anything, besides their so-called common knowledge approach, is impossible. Well, it is up to the individual to decide for themselves. The individual accepts that basic patterns, which shape the world, will decide what is true. If one person tells another that they are a horse, then they are not a horse. However, if a second person tells the same one that they are a horse, they are probably still not a horse, but if yet a third person tells the same one that they are a horse. Well, then that person better get a saddle, because they are a horse. This is the classic example of peer pressure, and it is used to shape a fictional reality; oppressing alternative viewpoints into submission. However, a different saying is much more reasonable. If it looks like a duck, walks like a duck, and talks like a duck, then it's a duck. Either, a person can believe what the brainwashed crowd says, or they can believe their own eyes.

Looking at the general nature of mounds and ruins, those of South America are in much better shape than those of North America. This is a common occurrence with enough time. Ruins abandoned hundreds of years ago, when made from stone, are often well enough preserved to hold a cohesive structure; like Mayapan and Machu Picchu. However, should that same structure have been abandoned many thousands of years ago, it would appear as no more than a mound. This same fact can be seen with similar buildings in Asia and Europe. Yet, an allegedly intellectual few would have us believe that the continents of North and South America defy this instance, and are extremely special. In fact, there are many more instance of illogical inconsistencies in dates, timelines, nature, and cultural backgrounds that plague our historical texts. Unfortunately, would anyone question this narrative, they are ridiculed for pushing alternative history, and lumped in with historical fiction writers. We are not allowed to question history, or we are threatened with ridicule, and much more. We must pretend to believe, and deny our own perception, for the vary mention of a dangerous subject could cost us money, time, and even our lives. However, should we allow an unquestioned fiction to continue, we will lose all of those anyway. It is extremely important for an individual to understand these subjects, and not be afraid to pursue them.

The dog men of Egypt and Mexico are one such subject that can cause danger to one's own life. A dog man is often thought of as a shape shifter. However, there are many more plausible explanations to this trope. Allegedly, the ancient cultures of Egypt and Mexico had no contact, at least until the glory of Europe arrived to its shores. However, there are far too many similarities among the gods Anubis and Xolotl. Among many other stark similarities between the ancient Egyptian and Aztec cultures, their two dog headed gods share the same responsibilities. Another aspect of these two gods is their depictions: male bodies crowned by a long snouted, pointy eared and black, dog head. Furthermore, the two bare the exact same shape. Now, returning to our dog breed, the xolotzcuintli canine appears as logical influence for both gods. Despite there being no reported xolotzcuintlis in Egypt, the god Anubis appears closer to this canine, rather than the different dogs provided: The Egyptian Jackal or Golden Wolf. As an added note, the Jackal and Golden Wolf appear more as coyotes of North America, rather than the figure of Anubis. Now, there is a strangely aggressive denial of these obvious facts, and an adamant certainty that world travel did not exist before the great age of exploration. This could be old propaganda, from a previous age, but it is strange that it persists so vehemently today.

Two more subjects that are aggressively unquestionable, which could possibly lead to fatal consequences, are the Nazi, or Socialist, and Communist concepts. Despite the fact that there is little difference between either, any deviation from the standard narrative will be met by harsh reactions. Simply speaking about these areas logically can bring physical violence to the argument, or even governmental crackdowns. This shows a great fear for these subjects, and being seen for what they are. Communist Socialism, or the Nazi Ideology, involves citizens that are made by and for the state.

Essentially, in this system, people are slaves to the state, and their lives are at its mercy. Of course, in this system the state runs everything, and governs every aspect of its subjects. There is no such thing as a private life in this system, and something as basic as marriage will require the state's authorization. Yet, we are only allowed to look at socialism through the microscopic lens of the Third Reich, and we are only allowed to say that the Nazis lost, as did the Communist Soviet Union. The twin concepts of State Socialism and Communism died with those two countries, and oppression no longer exists; at least, this is the only reality that we are allowed to say.

Now, onto the next dangerous subject, the Separatist War of these United States of America, commonly referred to as the U. S. Civil War. This war's title is only one aspect about this period that is illogical. First, we should understand what a civil war actually is. An internal conflict, a civil war is fought between two factions in the same government, for the same government. However, a separatist war would be fought between an entity that seeks to detract itself, and form its own government; as an independent entity. The Southern Confederacy of States sought to separate itself from the Union. Thus, they fought a separatist war, for separation. Furthermore, the only allowed narrative, with penalty of a governmental crackdown, or threats upon one's person, is that the so-called civil war was fought over the concept of slavery. Such individuals, that push this narrative, would have you deny your own logical brain, and vilify all the people of the Southern States. In fact, Shelby Foote, the leading mind on this subject, stated that he would fight for his native Kentucky, on the side of the South. Essentially, he stated that he would fight for a nation of alleged slave lovers. He would fight for a people that valued everything abhorrent to American values, and the warriors of the south valued slavery over their very own lives. So, many millions died in this war, but to protect the slave plantations of a privileged few. Naturally, this narrative makes no logical sense, like most that is taught in our indoctrination mills: public school. Furthermore, if the enforced narrative is true, then why is Shelby Foote the leading voice behind this period, since he would be a slave loving traitor, after all. Meanwhile, the true motive behind the U. S. Separatist War is one of the most obvious, and as old as time itself. The war was fueled by a desire for expanded power and money. It was fought between the cotton magnates of the Confederacy and the industrialists of the northern Union. The industrialists of the northern states depended on the southern monopoly for their cotton, so too did Great Britain. Therefore, the industrialists of the north, and Britain, resented the high prices that southern cotton growers charged. Instigated by the Central Banking System, the separatist southern states war of defense was doomed to fail, as their cotton was just too valuable for the northerners, and Britain. Of course, neither side was right in this fight, and neither side was wrong. The Union and the Confederacy lost, equally. In fact, it was a central bank that won, ran by oligarchs on the other side of the Atlantic. Furthermore, while the great figure of President Lincoln could not be removed, the reason for his fame could be obfuscated. Instead of allegedly freeing the slaves, a governmentally imposed tagline, President Lincoln was a great leader for his struggle against the central banking system. There is far more corroborating proof to this tale, than the state sanction, slimly proven, narrative; of a war fought solely over slavery. In addition, the victorious white men of the north descended south to free the poor black southern slave. This is, in fact, one of the most racist narratives that could be taught, and it is accepted by most. Essentially, the black slave was incapable of freeing themselves. So, they needed a white bureaucrat to do it; what a joke. Any alternative to this fiction is silenced, and justified as rebellious, racist, or white supremacist propaganda; or whatever other nonsensical label they would apply. Proof matters little, in this context, as any detraction will be met with a myriad of consequences. First, a person could be charged with a hate crime, or any number of arbitrary laws; passed by a clearly fascist and communist government. Additionally, such a person will be branded as a racist, and barred from living normal life, within the society that these arbiters control. Finally, an offender can be slain with impunity, for their bigoted racism. Therefore, the narrative, racist itself, that all the southern black slaves were freed by the white man, persists. When, in fact, we have all become slaves to these people. Black, white, brown, yellow, purple, blue, or any other color, all of us are slaves to the banking oligarchs, and the state. Even the birds and the bees come under their domain, and we all live in a fantasy of choice, or freedom.

Finally, questions and theories of any kind, no matter how small, will be met with harsh suppression. This begins in the state's propaganda system known as school, which is run by the Department of Education. All of these subjects are dangerous because they are carefully concocted fictions, designed to keep people mentally weak. As long as no one questions the narrative, then no one will seek the logical and rational truth. As long as all are afraid of reprisal, none will dare speak out against the state. Furthermore, we can be allowed our fantasy of freedom and liberty, as long as we dare not think liberally. If we begin to think, then we begin to question, and we will discover all of the lies that have been forced upon us. Unfortunately, today, there is little in the way of options, as it pertains to life at large. There is little choice for an alternative lifestyle. Fortunately, it is not impossible for an individual that questions the narrative to live, but it is very difficult. This is often referred to as persecution, which is the very thing the Nazis of the Third Reich are reported to have done, but they were defeated long ago; right? All of this is to say, understand which subjects are dangerous, and, if you want to live a peaceful life, never question the common narrative of these topics. Remember, we live in the time when Sauron rules.

Dances with Barbarians

The Hunter Gatherer is an idea that was formed by the global propaganda machine. It is a direct creation of a sedentary society, which is lauded as the most noble of pursuits, but only if the sedentary person follows the guidelines that are imposed. The subject, a child in this case, is passed through elementary school, and onto high school. During this process, they are taught that they came from hunter gatherers, but evolved into more sophisticated and proper creatures. Afterwards, once this idea has been cemented into the subconscious, all things that point to this past cultures is abhorred, as the hunter gatherer is akin to a Neanderthal, who does not possess the ability of speech. Therefore, all those that practice a hunter gatherer like lifestyle are ridiculed and persecuted; mainly by the brainwashed agents of schools, universities, television, and newspapers. The joint concepts of Neanderthals and hunter gatherers is a well-developed fiction, which took generations to solidify. The so-called creationists also push the fiction, while posing as an opposing force. This process took a lot of effort and tenacious solidification. So, the question must be asked, why go through all of the trouble? Furthermore, one might ask, where is the true opposition to this fiction. Well, it is simple, the opposition never left. Instead, rather than seeing themselves as an opposition, the hunter gatherer will live life, outside of modern society. As they ignore the state, and life outside of its confines, those that seek greater control despise these independent spirits. The fictions of outlaw criminals were invented to mobilize brainwashed

agents against those of an alternative lifestyle, and to steal
land. The Wild West is one of these fictions, used to expand
power, and is often applied to anything outside of state
control; which, by extension, is outside the control of
banking oligarchs. Now, here, we see why the hunter
gatherer fiction and Neanderthal are so heavily enforced.
When individuals practice a hunter gatherer lifestyle, such as
nomadic hunting cultures, they become independent;
something abhorred by the dominating and oppressive
society of modern times. While these aggressively controlling
individuals promote the sedentary culture, over the nomadic
hunter gatherer kind, they do not actually value sedentary
culture. The sedentary society is ideal for those that seek to
control and dominate others, because sedentary people do
not travel, and therefore do not experience other areas of the
world. Those who do not travel, and develop experience, are
easier to control, which is why the school system removed
practical application, long ago, especially in the areas of
linguistics and anthropology. In a controlled environment
people will believe anything that they are told, but, allow
them to venture into a completely separate environment, and
they will begin to compare their reality to those of others. In
fact, as the domineering arbiters of modern society project
their own sins onto others, they call those of independent
spirit barbarian and uncivilized. In this context, the saying
about pointing fingers, with three pointing back, is highly
applicable. When force, threats, and violence are used to
bend people into obedience, barbarism is being practiced. In
fact, there is no culture more barbaric and unsophisticated
than what is promoted by the school system, governments,
and other arbiters of modern society. They are ruthless and

murderous, and will do whatever it takes to expand their control, until all the world has been consumed by their hatred for freedom and independence.

The nomadic influence can be seen in the areas of the globe that are more free and independent. As nomads travel continuously, they depend on their own ingenuity and understanding to survive. Therefore, the nomadic culture is the antithesis to one of sedentary control. Now, when finding the nomadic influence, certain cultures stand out. In fact, when looking at physical characteristics, the ceremonial dress of the Osage people shows a direct connection to the people of the Eurasian steppes. Here, the similar dress, of peoples that supposedly never knew one another, can clearly be seen. Furthermore, there are ingrained cultural similarities between the people of Mongolia and the Osage Nation. With some true and in-depth research, a person might find the same similarities with other peoples of North America. However, these similarities stop as the American cultures move into the territory of the Aztec people. Now, on the subject of the Osage-Mongolian heritage, there is one important similarity that exists between them. The Osage and Mongolians refer to land as an ocean. As Tolkien referred to his world as Middle Earth, the Osage, or WhaZhaZhe, refer to themselves as the people of the middle waters. Additionally, the Mongols always referred to the steppe as the great ocean. Therefore, the similarities between these two cultures are unquestionable, and very apparent.

Now, we will move onto the similarities between Osage and Christian cultures, as naming all that exist between them and the Mongols would take a long time. In fact, the spirit of independence that exists in North America comes directly from the nomadic and self-reliant roots of the continent. The Osage believe in the great man of mystery, who created all the world, while the Christians believe in god, who created all the world. Furthermore, as we are all made in god's image and likeness, we are all little men of mystery. Therefore, it is no surprise that the cultures of Europe and the Americas worked so well together. There was a great amount of intermarriage among the European and American, and one of the most famous creations of these unions, the voyagers, is almost completely forgotten. Much of our history can still be found, but placed within a cesspool of obfuscation and misrepresentation. The true narrative is greatly problematic for those few that wish to bring society, and history itself, under their control. Instead, according to the fiction of the propaganda system, the so-called Indians, or Indigenous, of the North American continent died from disease, as they were hunter-gatherer barbarians, incapable of simple hygiene. Instead of admiring one's past ancestors, the propaganda systems teach us that those of the past were ignorant and slovenly. The great European culture was far superior, and supplanted that of the old. However, nothing could be further from the truth, as the people of Europe fled these very same arbiters of truth, for cultures that promoted individuality, personal responsibility, and self-directed independence. When it comes to these myths from the propaganda system, the founding of the government of these United States is always based in Roman and Greek culture. They would never allow the true origins of the government to be explored, as ancient Greek and Roman culture are paragons of the communist and socialist ideal.

Meanwhile, the Prussian and Germanic identity, another subject despised by the Greco-Roman propagandists, project their own socialist and controlling nature onto these long and forgotten concepts. In fact, the Prussians and Germanic people had a lot in common with those of the Northern Americas. While Prussia is taught as a state with an army, this state was able to stand-up to the controlling global system of European socialism. In fact, they even threw their king out of the country, after he was found to be traitor to the people. Furthermore, the Dithmarschen Republic was used as a rallying cry for a return to an independent German identity. Just as the influence of the noble savage sparked an outcry of independence in revolutionary France, so did the Dithmarschen Republic act as an ideal for the oppressed people of Central Europe. This rallying cry was then applied to Joseph Goebbels, as part of his Nazi propaganda. However, this makes little logical sense, as it directly opposes the ideal of domineering state control. Without an understanding of the basis for individual liberty, with personal responsibility as the driving force, many of the European people failed to gain their independence. This is because it is not something that is fought for, at least not with flesh and blood. Personal independence comes from a refusal to bow to the state, and by turning one's back on the lies of school teachers, movies, news articles, and politicians. Furthermore, slavery is only allowed to persist through the consent of the enslaved. Somewhat as a proverb, an Osage warrior was captured by a garrison of Spaniards, when the area was allegedly controlled by the Spanish crown. However, valuing his freedom over anything else, it took the entire garrison to hold the single Osage warrior. After multiple escape attempts, he eventually died from sustained wounds. This warrior would rather die than be held a prisoner, which is a perfect example of what personal independence means. If all refuse to be slaves, then it is impossible to hold any. An added note, the U. S. Marine Corps, also, teaches this concept; to never give up, or give in. The Marine Corps teaches to always attempt escape from a captor, until the last breath.

The concept of sedentary society is another fiction, proposed by the propaganda system of today. Remaining in the same place for an entire life time is unnatural, and they even have a word for what happens when people force themselves to live in the same place. A mid-life crisis is an ideal linked directly to the concept of a sedentary society. However, this is something pushed by the propaganda outlets as a negative outcome, one which should be avoided. There are so many mechanisms to keep people in the same place, for their entire lives; such as the concept of a career. However, this unnatural lifestyle will always cause pain, as the desire of freedom and independence is one of the strongest forces in our souls. People are only held in a career or location through fear, enforced by social pressure and even threat of prison. However, once again, all of these unnatural pressures will eventually be met by strong rebellion. On the other hand, when we examine the nomadic cultures, the systems of oppression have little or no effect, as can be seen with the so-called Spanish occupation of the Missouri and Mississippi regions. The Spanish had no effect on the locals, in the region called Louisiana, which was much larger than the state of Louisiana. While the Spanish saw the Osage as rebellious subjects, the Osage only viewed the

Spanish as a minor nuisance. Eventually, unable to make any headway with the Osage, the region was re-sold to the French, who, in-turn, sold it to the newly formed U. S. Government. In fact, when we look at this example, the Osage themselves produced the cause of their own demise, as the anti-European Arkansas bands fought with the Big Sky people, over-control of the old bloated Osage government. Finally, having decimated themselves, the bulk of the Osage sold their land, and bought territory in Oklahoma. The Osage had bought their new territorial lands, with the money that came from selling their empire, unlike most nations that formed treaties. Having struck oil on this new land, but legally purchasing it, the corrupt people in the U. S. Government were unable to push the Osage off this new territory. Still coveting the Osage holdings, many in the U. S. Government sanctioned assassinations against the Osage people, in a tale as old as time itself. This was the period called the Years of Fear. Absolute state control over the people was finally established in the 1920s, through the formation of the Federal Bureau of Investigation; which is, itself, an illegal organization. The Federal Bureau of Investigation contradicts everything that our union of countries, or states, was founded on. However, they were formed for our protection, or was it the protection of the Osage, because I forget.

Additionally, the modern world was logically established by three key groups, a fact that most of today's authoritarian regimes have erased from memory. Few of history's so-called facts make logical sense. Those that truly established the concept of freedom would never be promoted by a system that hates the constitution. One cornerstone of our values stems from smugglers, especially those in the 18th century. While the monopolies of European crowns practiced absolute control on paper, the majority of private businessmen ran smuggled goods. A number of smugglers were hanged as pirates, while a number of pirates were employed to stop smuggling. In fact, this is the very origin of the coast guard, having roots in the privateers of the Spanish crown. While these smugglers despised the state, which sought only to control the people, they had no real way to resist such organizations, and that is where Prussia comes in. Despite their linking to Nazi organizations, and being only remembered as the backbone of the Third Reich, in Winston Churchill's words, the sovereign nation state of Prussia was the backbone of revolution. The U. S. Military war manual, from our own revolution, was written by a Prussian general, named Freidrich Wilhelm von Steuben. In addition, Emil Korner was Prussian general that trained the troops of revolutionary Chile. While Prussia has all but been forgotten, as the mold for Hitler's Gestapo, they are truly hated, by the self-styled ruling class, for their efforts in the revolutionary period of world history. Moving away from the Prussian example, the last and final element that sparked revolution was that of the noble savage. While traveling, as a delegation to France, Osage representatives spoke with multiple French writers and figures of importance. Thus, the idea of representative government, and self-governance, came to be. The Iroquois Federation, and many other groups, gave similar lessons, but the make-up of parliament is directly, and obviously, based on the old government of the Osage Empire. The Isolated Earth and Big Sky people formed two camps within the old Osage Nation, which could be akin to the rival political parties of today. Like today, these two groups eventually came to work together, secretly of course. However, the important fact here is that the Osage had representative chieftains, who only held power based on their number of followers. The saying in the Osage Nation is that people vote with their feet, meaning the destination, where the people walked, would represent their decisions. The main representative of the nation was picked from these chieftains, whichever had the majority of followers. Now, it is important to note that the Osage Nation's main representative did not have the power to make war. Rather, that responsibility lay with a separate body of elders, known as the Little Men of Mystery. When this counsel called war, all Osage of fighting ability were called up, in order to rain down hell onto those that declare war on the Nation; as in the case of an Osage boy that was ambushed. To explain the importance of this event, an individual war band leader could make their own decisions, and every individual was left to face the consequences to their own actions. However, retribution against an Osage, that had nothing to do with the crime of another, was considered an act of war against all Osage The boy was killed for the actions of another Osage, as retribution. Unfortunately, for those that killed the boy, the wrath of the entire nation was brought to bear. Now, all Osage were considered of fighting ability, and all had a shared responsibility to defend one another, but there was no punishment for ignoring the call to war. Instead, those that answered the call were given an elevated position in society. In this example, the chieftain that lead the destruction of the offenders, became known as four lodges. This name related to his action, because he led his men to all four lodges of the enemy, and killed all men, women, children, and animals therein. To declare war on the Osage, meant all of their enemy would die, or they would: this is called total war. Now, these three cornerstones, the influence of the noble savage, the Prussian general, and the smuggler, established a world of freedom and independence that is mostly forgotten. Finally, further evidence of the manipulation of the historical narrative can been seen in population counts. There is a heavy bias in the death counts that were written by Muslim scholars, about the Mongolian conquests. Naturally, there is, also, a European centric bias in historical battle estimates. The contrast in numbers, between combatant counts in the Americas, versus those in Europe, is staggering. In fact, they would have us believe that the military professionals of the time were unaware of what constituted a major battle, versus a minor and unmentionable skirmish. Rather than delving into the specific numbers, which takes a simple comparative search, examining this objectively and reading between the lines gives an obvious explanation. The influence of rebellious savage nations causes the European to despise the American. As European nobility despises being thought of as weak, their bias will manifest in high population and troop counts, on paper. Reporting severely bloated numbers, for European battles, would be a representation of their strength. Meanwhile, the low combatant counts in the early north American continent would show our weakness. In the European centric mind, which adores the feudal system, and abhors individual liberty, the greatest insult to their pride and vanity is to mention their weakness. They are not victims, they victimize. They cannot be destroyed, since it is they that commit the genocide. The true threat to the power of our global overlords, which mainly come from a European banking nobility, is to be thought of as weak. If they are found to be weak, then they will become ignored, and irrelevant; a road that they are now on.

The Cloaked Daggers

Throughout history, the game of power has revolved around the control of information. The powers that be will use whatever tactics necessary to maintain their hold. An imbalance of control, or absolute dominance, will lead to taboo subjects. Harboring feelings of resentment, the taboo will be held up by those most mistreated and marginalized, these subjects will be established as ideals, which will allow for little objective thought. These banned ideas will provide a rallying banner for marginalized groups, while the current authority will seek to burn this banner. Should the resentful rise and become victorious, they will inevitably cast down the previous regime. Then, the fallen regime will be placed under the very same taboo that the resentful previously occupied. Subsequently, history will become obscured by separate factions, attempting to wrestle control from one another, and make war in the arena of knowledge. The work of truth seekers becomes increasingly important in this regard. Should truth be allowed to fall into obscurity, worse outcomes will take place. Additionally, actionable intelligence will become a forethought, and the ignorance will become the standard, leading to mutual chaos and destruction.

While often these changes of power are scene as products of society, there are always parallel societies whose actions are rarely understood by the surface one. Many names exist for parallel societies, and the underworld is often the name chosen for the criminal one. More often than not, the secret societies are those parallel ones, where laws and government are seen as the proving grounds. Within these societies, groups will fight for power, which is what leads to collateral damage in the public society. Therefore, the antithesis to the current secret group in power will be the underworld, criminalized by the secret groups that runs things currently. Many secret groups may be pushed into the underworld, while others are brought into the main parallel. While both societies depend on the main one, which is often referred to as public opinion, the two continuously compete in the shadows. Should the underworld, or secret society, become completely understood by the public, it would become very dangerous to the existence of every group involved. However, this danger generally does not lie with the public, but rather rival parallel societies. Through the public's discovery, one group might become open for invasion from another. In this subject, the parallel society is not a single group. After-all, if we think about what a society is, multiple groups are often involved. Therefore, conspiracy theories often only scratch the surface, and what we consider secret societies are, actually, only groups. We can examine this distinction between society and group in the subject of the so-called Prohibition Era. At this time, the New York Italian Crime families formed a secret society of intrigue, but their society was the antithesis to the clandestine ones that controlled the government. Therefore, the entire criminal society of bootleggers and thugs all shared a common code; which involved never speaking to the police, as the police forces were often the agents of the parallel society that controlled government. It should be of noted that bootleggers often trusted and worked with sheriffs. This is because sheriffs are elected by the people, while the police stem from city councils, or the federal government. Now, with those two definitions simply understood, we shall cover the subject of important secret groups.

The White Lotus consisted of Chinese agents that sought to reestablish the Han dynasty, and their presence can still be felt today. However, many of the members of this organization would not consider themselves Chinese. Furthermore, they do not fit the definition of a society, as they are a single group, with a shared goal. While the group may contain factions within their organization, they cannot be considered a society. On the other hand, they do share space with other secretive groups in the Nation State of China; including the Triads. While much of this is already known, it takes a perceptive mind to study and understand history, see the logical outcomes, and notice the signs and symbols. In addition, the Nizari Ismaelis make a perfect example of a secret group that helped shape the landscape of the world. While this group was not the only one to open the gates of Eurasia, for the conquests of Genghis Khan and his dogs of war, they were a major player in this arena. Also, the Nizari Ismaeli group established the famous middle eastern tactic of threatening royalty and governmental officials, rather than threatening the public at large. Conversely, threats against the public, mass executions, and public executions, are all hallmarks of European governance. The great conquests of Genghis Khan, throughout the Middle East, came about due to instability in the region: instability that was created by assassinations from the Nizari Ismaeli. On the other hand, the major driving force behind the Mongol conquests came from the high nomadic slave populations throughout the area.

When it comes to the subject of Genghis Khan, and the
Mongol Empire, a few elements prove the true driving force
behind the inevitable campaigns of death and destruction.
First, the bloodthirst that the Mongols possessed for royalty,
seen in the demand letters and messages to such leaders,
show that these Mongols were on a quest. This quest was
fueled by hatred for slave masters. Timujin, or Genghis
Khan, was himself a slave, or, at least, such is conjectured by
the writer Jack Weatherford. This theory is very applicable, if
not applied to the extremely high levels of nomad slaves that
populated the regions of their conquest. However, Western
Europe contained lower nomadic populations than the
Eastern portion, and the Middle East. Furthermore, Africa
contained very few nomadic slaves, although modernist
history would say the Mongols were stopped by the
Mamelukes, slave soldiers that also rose to power.
Unfortunately for the modern narrative, there is only one
logical conclusion. The conquests came to an end when the
borders of the slave empire were reached. This is because the
nomad slaves would have been perfect sources of
intelligence for the Mongol forces, providing such secretive
information through poems. Completely forming evidence
for this matter would take some extensive research, but,
through logical analysis, we can find the proof in the big
picture. I would implore every person to do their own
research, because that which is presented can be false and
manipulated evidence. In addition to the subject of nomadic
slave populations, Western European culture was only saved
because the nomads were few in numbers there. Now, the
murder of Mongol envoys is likely a piece of propaganda,
perhaps even of the Mongols, because the narrative is

illogical. Why would anyone decide to work as an envoy, if they always return to the Khan in pieces. Furthermore, why would an envoy be sent to royalty, a status that was outlawed under Mongol edicts. A questioning mind is necessary in this regard, because so much propaganda surrounds the subject.

Few subjects, when it comes to secret societies, are still taboo today. However, the important ones will illicit ridicule and persecution, which shows the current effects of their influence. The Order of the Freemasons is an organization that openly operates, but, should they be analyzed, immediate wrath will be directed toward the offender, stemming from the modern societal systems. The group despises the outing of its members, as this could weaken the organization. A majority of so-called influential figures of today, and the past, have open membership in this group. Clearly, anyone with eyes in their head could see the touch of the group on politics, religion, entertainment, industry, and every level of the main modern society. Figures such as George Washington and Benjamin Franklin were freemasons, allegedly. Therefore, the question must be asked, were these men fiction, to push pro-freemason propaganda. Perhaps, none of these figures exist, their actions certainly do not promote a freedom loving objective. Maybe, if they did exist, their only influence was gained through their membership in the clandestine group. While this group is not the only one, others appear to hold even more power. Mere mention of the Rothschild banking clan, the classically named Illuminati, and others, can illicit more than simple ridicule. The names of these groups are only mentioned behind doors, and in hushed voices, because mentioning them openly could have the person labeled a conspiracy theorist, a charge worse than insanity, despite the illogical nature of the label.

The Sicilian Resistance forces compromise one of the most secretive and influential groups that made their unequivocal mark on history. Their touch can still be seen in the city of Las Vegas, Chicago, New York, and Hollywood. The island of Sicily, constantly being invaded by foreign powers, formed some of the most successful resistance fighters in history; and eventually became known as the Italian Mafia. Despite their Sicilian origins, the Italian Mafia became far more powerful in the United States of America then they ever were in their home country. Originally, forming as an organization to fund the resistance families in Sicily, the New York organizations of the Italian Mafioso became La Cosa Nostra, which broke from their fathers in the home country; at least, it was reported as such. These resistance groups found a home among the freedom loving and rebellious citizen of the United States of America; back when the spirit of freedom was strong among the people. A brutal crackdown by a traitorous and authoritarian government, the era of prohibition saw much expansion through violence against the people. Therefore, the organization of the Mafia came about, as an antithesis to the federal government, which had sold itself long ago. Most people ignored the laws by the U. S. Government, which led to mass raids and expansion of the Federal Bureau of Investigation, but the Mafia stepped in to corrupt these very organizations that sought to shut them down. In fact, logically, the only thing that actually stopped the mafia can be seen in the licensing of gambling. While the repeal of the Prohibition Act had little effect on the mafia, as they were heavily involved in other illicit activities, the licensing of gambling, and other such nefarious desires, would place all the power squarely in the hands of the federal government, once more. On the other hand, as Las Vegas has long been the only center of legal prostitution, the hand of the Italian Mafia can still be seen; although many other groups had a hand in this. In fact, it was the first televised hearing before congress that established the Italian mafia as the face of the underworld, and the mafia bosses that presented themselves. Therefore, due to these aspects, was this all a propaganda fiction, using a publicized dog and pony show to push the idea of the Mafioso, and remove the place of the rebellious American citizen. Such an occurrence would not be the only time. After all, there is nothing the state hates more than a free and independent citizen, because such a person could completely undermine their control. Instead, the mafia served two purposes, threaten the public, and remove the prominence of the American bootlegger.

The Venetian Banking Clans are old families that still hold immense power, as their names are even less known, when compared to their counter-parts. If a person speaks about the Freemasons they will likely be laughed at, and if the person talks about the Rothschild and Illuminati they could lose their jobs, but delving into the venetian banking clans could put a person in the ground. When compared to the body count that was linked to the Clintons, the one linked to the Venetian banking clans could be numbered in the billions. As with any secret society, the only true information that can be found is through the analysis of patterns and extensive research. However, as the clans still hold immense power, actually acting on any derived information could prove dangerous. These clans could be linked to the Vatican archives, the U. S. Separatist War, establishing of central banks, the funding of global organizations, the placements of politicians, kings, queens, and the removal of such. In fact, the assassinations of Lincoln and his cabinet members could be traced back to these clans. However, as listing all of the rabbit holes would take ages, leaving this subject up to the professionals would be wise. However, the Venetian rabbit hole is very long and winding.

The Yakuza have a lot in common with the Italian Mafia of Sicily and the United States of America. Also forming as an underground resistance force, many of the Yakuza clans can trace ancestry back to the Samurai clans of the Shogunate. With the increased influence of western banks, and the secret societies that came with them, the old samurai clans had to defend their position. Unfortunately, they had been supplanted, and became the antithesis to the new power. Of course, the Yakuza really did not take their true form until after the pacific campaign, in the so-called Second World War, when the western banking system was imposed on the island country. In this accord, Japan was handed a near monopoly on electronic goods, as planned by the banking clans and secret groups that quietly run the world, and quietly intrigue and war against one another. Just as with our example of the mafia, the question should be posed, is the origin of the Yakuza real, or are they simply another propagandized figment; which removes the role of an important historical group? When it comes to the smugglers of the 18th century, such a large economic resistance to the royalist state cannot be mentioned in history texts.

Therefore, the pirate became a focus point, to obfuscate from the role of the smuggler. The same can be seen with the CIA backed gangs of Los Angeles, and the drug cartels of South and Central America, in addition to those of Mexico. Now, the secret groups establish absolute power of the citizens, placing such between a rock and a hard place. The state controls both the legal and illegal mechanisms, bring money in from both ends. In fact, taxes are collected from all sources, and funnel back to the central banking systems. It is relatively simple, and many of these groups must be questioned, because a majority are objects of the state, and the clandestine groups that run the state.

The Hidden Leaves

The Alphabet Company is possibly even more of a joke than the Agenda 21. While the overlords of the world lay out their plan for world domination in a world summit in Brazil, the hilariously named Alphabet Company carries out their diabolical plans. In fact, the placement of the Alphabet Company in the world is so obvious, and in our faces, that it is a miracle more people do not see them for who they are; the federal government. The explanation for this can be found with the U. S. federal agencies that carry out the bidding of global oligarchs. Also, an internet meme will help us explain the nature of the Alphabet Company. Almost every agency in the Federal Government can be referred to by a series of letters. Thus, they are often called the letter agencies. The Federal Bureau of Investigation is often abbreviated to the FBI, while the Central Intelligence Agency can be named the CIA. Additionally, the National Security Agency is referred to as the NSA, the Internal Revenue Service is the IRS. The Department of Homeland Security is the DHS. Along with the DEA, ATF, and DOJ, the majority of Federal Agencies are referred to as Letter Agencies. Furthermore, the companies of Marines, Sailors, Soldiers, and Airmen, that staffed the military support for a few of these agencies were called letter companies. Now, the internet meme that perfectly explains the relationship of these agencies to the Alphabet Company, which runs Google and its affiliates, is based in the Boogaloo meme. Truly instilling fear in these authorities of life, truth, and the pursuit of happiness, the boogaloo began as a joking reference to the second civil war, at least that is how it is reported. Now, just to be technical, the boogaloo, within the meme, would be the First Civil War, because what is referred to as the U. S. Civil War was a Separatist War. Continuing with the earlier topic, were an individual to join one of these boogaloo groups, primarily on Facebook, a variety of characters could be found. As this subject will be covered later in the book, the only applicable reference here is how the Boogaloo Bois, a term for the members of these groups, refer to the ATF and FBI no-knock raids; as being carried out by Alphabet Bois, and blowing up these Federal Agents makes Alphabet soup. If an explanation of a no-knock raid is necessary, it is when government agents arrive to serve a warrant that requires no identification by the officers involved, and does not actually require federal involvement, but is mostly used in relation to the seizure of firearms. Without going into an analysis of the moral and ethical implications, or effectiveness of the strategy, the no-knock raid clearly does not represent the will of the people. Now, if I have to explain the connection further, between the fictional federal agent alphabet boys in a meme, and the real Alphabet Company that runs Google, and affiliates, then most of this book can be compared to a tree, who tries to relate to an arctic seal.

Narrative control is a particularly old aspect of the federal control system, which governs the rebellious peasant slave subjects throughout most of North America. Mostly governed under jurisdiction of the Central Intelligence Agency, and their operation mockingbird, the same strategy of narrative control is practiced globally, at this point. While the Central Intelligence Agency's Operation Mockingbird can be a starting point, to understand how narrative control takes place, it only scratches the surface of this global phenomenon, and relies on a few key aspects. First, logical dissent must be quickly and brutally crushed, and this can be accomplished in a number of ways, with the methods of bullying and peer pressure being the most reliable. However, this control was established through painstaking effort. Under the guise of combating communism, under Operation Mockingbird, the Central Intelligence Agency established their own Iron Curtain of Communist Propaganda; at least, communist in practice, but not in name. This took place mainly through bribery, admitted to by the agency, but they likely employed any tactic that worked. Thus, control over media outlets came under absolute control of the state, all for the sake of national security and combating communism. While the effects of Operation Mockingbird persist today, the influence has moved into more spheres than just news articles and Hollywood. The control of the narrative takes place in many ways. However, the strategies are fairly straightforward. If news comes out that greatly damages the ruling class, like child trafficking in Hollywood, the propaganda outlets will push a different story that proves much more manageable. This tactic can be seen in the clearly scripted response of the actor Brad Pitt, when talking about Pedophilia in Hollywood. Brad Pitt stated the pedophilia takes place in Hollywood, but it is mostly the responsibility of the parents, who desired stardom for their children, at any cost. It is much easier to manage a story of parents that will do anything, to place their children into the spotlight, including subjecting them to pedophilia by rogue agents. Alternatively, managing the story of rampant child trafficking, prostitution, and slavery, with most being forced against the will, is much harder to control. It is also easier to place blame among the parents, than talk about adrenochrome, taken from the adrenaline that is produced by children; while the child is subjected to torture. While this example is in the extremely, it perfectly describes narrative diversion and management, a hallmark of the Central Intelligence Agency's narrative control. There is much more that goes into the strategy of narrative control, and many more tactics, but the main objective is pretty straightforward; do whatever it takes to retain control of the narrative. It doesn't matter what is reported, or what is believed, as long as control of the narrative is retained, and people only discuss what they are permitted to. Now, Diverting Perspective is another famous tactic, and should be one of note. When bad news comes out, that makes the global overlords appear weak, the propaganda machine will bring attention to a separate story. Thus, they divert attention away from the problematic story. This can be seen in the example of the NIXVM sex cult, which is a much easier story to manage than a member of the British royal family being involved in a scandal that involves the trafficking and prostitution of children. Therefore, the use of news stories about the sex cult can divert attention away from their more hideous crimes.

Now, to explain some less extreme examples, and how the influence of the Central Intelligence Agency can be seen in the most mundane areas, we will examine the 2015 movie *Goosebumps*. In the opening scenes, the main character, a teenager, arrives in an unnamed suburb, which is clearly populated by the upper echelons of society, or individuals that have incurred a lot of debt; as many of the houses would be in the six figures. However, the main character creates many names for this place, even referring to it as North Korea, and he would rather return to New York city. Now, as anyone who has traveled knows, any metropolis is dirty, grimy, and dangerous. The location for this opening scene is much nicer than any city, let alone New York City. Why would such a clear disparaging remark be made? The answer is simple, subliminal messaging for the purpose of urbanization. The corrupt oligarchs wish to push all citizens into the major cities, so more control can be implemented; and the idea of the superiority of the city is submerged in the subconscious at an early age. In conjunction with their plans for increased urbanization, the oligarchy also wishes to push people away from driving, which is why the implement efforts to make driving in their control centers more and more difficult. Increased parking costs, taxes, and paid parking on every block, will guide people away from vehicles, and onto so-called public transportation. Now, as this subject moves onto seizure of travel outlets, a topic covered later, we shall continue with the mockingbird theme. When it comes to famous people, no matter who they are, if their fame was gained through the system, then they are objects of it. Figures such as Ayn Rand and Jordan Peterson are clear agents of the Central Intelligence Agency. As all true threats are ruthlessly suppressed, any that are allowed to see the light of day can be seen as they agents; but parading as the opposition. This can also be applied to the Anarchist Cookbook and Rules for Radicals. There will be just enough pushback to make their double agents appear legitimate, but they are all made for narrative control. Furthermore, the works of George R. R. Martin, as they are reported, stink like a dead fish in summer. This is because all of the propaganda outlets say that his alleged works were based off the War of the Roses in history. However, clear symbolism in the book contradicts this, as there are clear links to the history of Eastern Europe. Now, why would the system hate these stories so much? Apart from the rampant pedophilia among the royal characters in the book, they are also depicted as slovenly, childish, and, most importantly, weak. Now, apart from shutting down, adopting into their control, or diverting attention away from their rivals, the CIA's narrative control can be seen in other ways. Never will a character in a propaganda piece be seen as having a successful natural birth. Instead, all characters depend solely on the hospital, an institution of the oppressive system that we live under. A good way to recognized a propaganda piece, and paid opposition, is not to focus on what is said. Rather, the question should be asked; will this help, or hurt, their system?

Net neutrality, a concept that implements the opposite of what its name implies, was a series of propaganda pieces that established total authoritarian control over the internet, and cellular service. The governing body of all communication methods, in the United States, is the Federal Communications Commission. An organization that hampers and destroys all progress and innovation in the electronic field. Implementing net neutrality policies, without the backing of any actual laws, or consent of the people, the rogue Federal Communications Commission allowed for a rapid expansion by the Federal Governments corporation, the Alphabet Company, and solidified absolute control over the internet. Any dissenters were arrested and imprisoned for a myriad of crimes, and the very public prosecution of the Silk Road's Dread Pirate Roberts, which was widely publicized in the mockingbird media, was likely a narrative diversion to avoid notice of the FCC's takedown to expand the Alphabet Company's control. While net neutrality is the least of this agency's crimes, it did completely remove any anonymity of freedom that the internet brought to the people of the world. Although, not acting on behalf of the United States, the FCC did bring the protection of the internet under the control of our global nobility, as we peasants cannot be trusted with such a dangerous idea like anonymity, or freedom.

Moving on, when it comes to control through currency, we are all made into slave peasants; mostly regardless of choice. Any purchasing or bargaining that is done without the approved currency is brutally punished, and often called tax evasion. In fact, these people, that pretend to have our best interests at heart, couldn't care less about what happens to each and everyone one of us. We are just numbers on paper. So, expecting any sort of fair justice from them, and their agents, is the height of naivety. In the United States of America, the main mechanism in place for reaping the appropriate currency from the populace is the Federal Reserve, which uses the Department of Treasury and the Internal Revenue Service as their tax collecting thugs. Alternatively, the Federal Reserve also controls the currency, printing a finite quantity. Therefore, what they collect is based on what we are allowed to have, since we are peasants, they require us to be in a perpetual state of poverty; which is also a reason for inflation. However, rather than going into the specifics of the economic manipulation, they do all the work for us. Since we are not allowed to pay in gold or silver, we are forced to live in their system. Their business reports are known as Gross Domestic Products, and other economic numbers. Rather than the worthless currency that is forced on us, they trade in resources; including the human resource. Naturally, this group of people does not include their enforcement agents, who are also paid in worthless currency, but the individuals that attend world trade exchanges. They are the ones that go to the extremely boring meetings over GDP. Essentially, those that carefully pay attention to the shifts in GDP are often involved in this system, but might also be a slave peasant, who is aware of his plight. Finally, if you ever think that it might be easier just to work within the system, and keep your mouth shut, there is one question that you should ask yourself. How do you feel about being a peasant slave, with your destiny predetermined by a group of faceless overlords that meet in a board room, and discuss the blip on their piece of paper that is you?

Now, let us talk about the classic tactic of strategy and tactic control. Yes, that phrase was very convoluted, but it is accurate. The likes of Niccolo Machiavelli and Saul Alinsky are perfect examples of tactic controllers. Their books were meant to teach specific lessons on how to manipulate and gain power, which could simply be called control. However, their teachings were meant to cause us, the peasants, to use tactics that they could manage. After all, if we use the tactics that they teach us, then we won't be using such a problematic concept as creativity. While Machiavellian and Alinskian tactics can be effective, they are also easy to defeat, unlike an unknown and unnamed tactic, or strategy.

Therefore, by publishing and teaching certain tactics, other methods will not even be attempted. Just as the old concept of continuously repeating a subject until it becomes a law, Machiavelli and Alinsky, along with Hitler, are constantly mentioned. This has the effect of their works being pushed front and center in most, if not all, aspects of social interaction. While effective, this strategy is not full-proof, and still allows for creative and alternative solutions; to damage the influence of our global nobles. Unfortunately, they often pivot, having the control of the narrative, and control over the minds of the majority of the human populace. People such as Jordan Peterson and Alex Jones are agents of our nobility, while pretending to be the opposition, and this is generally referred to as paid opposition. These two figures have been mentioned and widely publicized by the outlets under the control of these nobles, like major news organizations. In fact, often agents can be detected by how well they are known, as the nobility would rather silence, or distract, from true threats to their power. The names of Jordan Peterson, Machiavelli, Alinsky, or Alex Jones would not be known, if they weren't agents of those people.

Instituting another tactic of subversive control, the Central Intelligence Agency sought to remove the bonds of family, but first they targeted community. One of these methods included the undermining of holidays. First, we should outline what a true holiday is, to understand the fake ones pushed by the mockingbird system. Along with a theme, a holiday must include activities that bring together the community. Stories, traditions, themes, locations, and beliefs are all necessary elements to make a true holiday. Now, let us examine the fake holidays that were instituted by the CIA, and their efforts to undermine the real ones. First, instead of Christmas, which was similar to the Winter Festival, being a community activity, it was made religious. Despite having nothing to do with the birth of Christ, Christmas became a time to be alone with one's family, locked inside and unable to do anything; which also contributed to their plans of breaking up family bonds. Now, while this happened before the technical formation of the CIA, the CIA is simply a continuing of similar groups. As one of their tactics is to constantly change the name of their same organization, after it comes under scrutiny. Moving on, there are a large number of fake holidays, created by the CIA. We should understand, using the example of a real holiday, how a lot of these holidays lack the elements of a holiday. The day of the woman, father, and mother are all CIA holidays. In addition, Kwanza is another CIA fabrication. Now, apart from the obvious benefits that these holidays give to CIA control, they also further obfuscate the importance of a holiday; dividing, rather than bringing together. Using our example of Christmas, a holiday that was invented for what used to be the dead of winter, people in the community would gather to share presents and festivities. The true purpose to a holiday is community engagement and light hearted bonding. Now, often, there was no specific day required to do this, but that fact differs between culture and time period. In a society dominated by overbearing overlords, the importance of a true holiday is never more needed. Together, with the support of a community, individuals feel belonging and happiness, but alone, and without the ability to engage with their community, people become sad and depressed; a perfect and malleable state for the oligarchs and their system. Furthermore, the random poisonings of food and delivery packages, at least publicized as such by the mockingbird media, people became distrustful of their neighbors; a tactic seen in publicized serial killers. After all, as stated in most movies and books of this genre, people often left their homes unlocked, before a catastrophe struck. In fact, there are many more methods that were implemented to destroy community bonds, but even more to destroy the family.

Now, there are many that pretend to be on the side of the people that will say America is under attack. They will say many rogue groups exist, seeking to tear down freedom, and the so-called social experiment of America. This is all part of the narrative control, but, reading between the lines, we can ascertain their true meaning. Naturally, these people are afraid of losing America, at least their America. The true origins of freedom from tyranny were lost long ago, when the Federal Government sold themselves to global entities in 1871; which is the year a treaty was signed with Great Britain. Of course, the not so Great Britain, has likely never been governed by its citizens, as they have been peasant slaves to their government for generations. Therefore, the fear of these people, in losing their America, is a direct representation of their waning power. Many of these authoritarian and murderous groups, imposing their sins on the general populace, are losing, which is why they cry and beg for us to defend their great social experiment of America, and their attempts to dominate all life.

The Great Cudgel

The Treaty of 1871 is when the last piece of the Americas was returned to a group of European oligarchs, and when traitorous politicians became the puppets of would-be tyrants; across the pond. Additionally, when a person thinks of war, the main theme that comes to mind is that of the so-called world wars. Despite the fact that these wars did not take place across the world, there is one element about these, different than others. At least as it is portrayed, the world wars claimed the lives of countless brave soldiers, mostly men. However, it is saddening and sickening to imagine how many died in every war that was not of their making. In fact, the majority of wars that U. S. citizens died in, were neither by, nor for, the people. Instead, their lives were used as pawns in a manufactured conflict. They were as the pieces on a chess board. Those that cared not for their lives, seeing them as expendable, are the vary individuals that ordered them across mined fields; such as the infamous no-man's land. Those few individuals, as we are led to believe, that have family that served in all the major wars, have lived a life a constant sadness and despair. So, it is difficult to say that many of them died as a cudgel for a privileged few, and not the unquestionable taglines of bravery and sacrifice. Were the individuals of these families able to glean the names, of those that had used their loved ones as play things, the justified reaction would be great indeed. However, this is a reaction that these global overlords do not fear, as they are masters of control through such an emotion. Instead, their greatest fear is to become irrelevant and ignored. Visualized weakness is their greatest fear.

Pearl Harbor was an event used to inspire a great war against the Japanese Imperial Nation, as it is called in the history books. A narrative was needed so that the treasonous federal government could bring the United States Military to bear, in their masters' desire for further control. While people need a cause to intervene in Europe, the same was necessary for Japan. Instead of being liberators, the United States military was used to place the citizens of the world in chains. However, manipulated, the United States military was one of the greatest cudgels in history, and solidified a dominant and worldwide banking system. As Japan was under an imperial system, they barred foreign banks from taking hold. This could not be allowed, because the European banking clans desired all the land in the world to be under their control. However, the banks, and their overlords, possessed the United States military, which was still robust. They could use this force against the Japanese. After all, the majority of their other forces had been used to suppress rebellions in Europe, and bring the continent under their absolute control. The only pieces they had left to play came from the Americas, and the United States had the best force to accomplish this goal. Whether or not a person believes in the current banking system, and how they manipulated the world into their control, the United States military was, undeniably, one of their main weapons that was used against the world. Instead of an American empire, as these people like to project onto the citizens of the continent, America is simply a pawn for a worldwide banking empire, one which cannot be destroyed through physical tactics alone.

While the incident at Pearl Harbor was used to inspire attacks against Japan, the 911 Attack was used to inspire attacks against Iraq and Afghanistan. However, as the banking clans and global traders prefer to kill multiple birds with one stone, the events of this period were used to silence dissenters, and threaten the entire globe into submission. After all, the Global War on Terror was global, and any that challenged the propagated narrative could be labeled extremists, and dealt with accordingly. The majority of global citizens went along with this, bowing to their overlords, and accepting their plight as obedient peasants. Unfortunately, for the Iraqis and Afghanis, the United States military was brought against them. Rather than being used against an oppressive regime, soldiers were ordered to guard and burn fields, and farmer's crops, while protecting the government that they had allegedly come to destroy. Of course, any dissenters within the ranks were quickly disposed of. In fact, the actions during this period did the most to unravel the fictional narrative, in the minds of those that mattered most. Along with Vietnam, veterans of the period, of the Global War on Terror, became aware of the game being played against them, but only a few understood just how much had been done under the guise of liberation, and how the most freedom loving force in the world had put the world in chains. Rather than defending, the military had been used to destroy and dominate the enemies of the privileged nobility. Countless lives were squandered like worthless pieces of currency. Now, those that said anything against these actions, whether in Vietnam, or Iraq, were immediately labeled and persecuted. On the other hand, these people miscalculated this time, making too many enemies, and allowing to many to travel and seek understanding, a fact that they are trying to alleviate with the proposed pandemic of 2020. There is much more that the United States has been used for in the subjugation of the world, especially embargos, but much of this can be found with objective understanding, and self-guided research. Searching for answers within the propaganda system is like asking a blind person to drive. Therefore, if this book can save a single person, from dying for a fake cause, then any consequence will be more than worth it; as they say, damn the consequences.

Now, the World Trade Centers play a major role in the expansion of global power. In addition to being hubs of trade expansion, the twin towers were twice used to inflict more suppression, and achieve greater control, against the citizens of the United States. Meanwhile, the United Nations, with the backing of their really big stick, the U. S. Military, expanded oligarchical control over the globe. While parading as saviors, the United Nations solidified control over the majority of Africa, South America, and other so-called "developing" nations. The United Nations sent in their forces to "keep the peace", and assist with "humanitarian aid." It was the classic excuse for absolute power and complete suppression, through the guise of increased safety and security for the populace. Essentially, the United Nations would label their enemies as dictators, and then fuel staged out-rage among the people, which was brought about through a myriad of ways; including threats against the populace through bombings, and invasions. Once the alleged dictator is removed, multiple groups are pitted against each other, to sew chaos and destruction. This is a prime example of conquest through division. Now, whether or not this takes place, the cabal's mockingbird media will make it so, through phony news stories, and mentioning the fake conflict through their so-called "popular culture" outlets. Celebrities, actors, singers, and other mouth pieces of the oligarchy will come out against the, United Nation accused, dictator. Then, their mouthpieces will speak out and condemn the violence that the media reports, whether real or imagined. Finally, the United Nations will send a force of aid workers into the problematic region. Thus, they will conquer the area, as liberating heroes, when they are, in fact, instilling themselves as absolute rulers. In the majority of places that the United Nation's assist, the lives of the citizens are worse off than before, even if a real dictator ruled. The same connection can be seen through Bill Gates, who controls the World Health Organization, and, by extension, all the Health Departments around the world, and the Center for Disease Control. The current plan that they are putting into effect now has been in the making for decades; apparent from fear mongering propaganda movies and video games. Finally, with the example of the world trade center towers, along with the strange, physics defying, circumstances around their destruction, multiple birds were killed with two planes, and a couple of bombs. The world trade center was bombed in 1993, a test run for the destruction of the buildings on September 11th. The destruction of evidence was one reasons for bringing these monolithic buildings down, apart from others, but it also fueled outrage from the public; a rage which was funneled towards the enemies of the United Nations, and their masters. In fact, there is so much that is suspect around this area that it would take many more pages to outline it all. However, while there are many other circumstances like this, events that are often referred to as false flags, the World Trade Center attacks did much to expand control of the global oligarchy, in the United States and abroad.

Protected Classes

When one thinks of a protected class, the rich often come to mind. While this is the narrative that is pushed by the propaganda outlets, it is only half true. Some of the wealthy are part of a protected class, but a protected class is not made by wealth. Instead, certain groups of people are vilified by the system, while others are beyond reproach. In this regard, truth is of little consequence, but reality can be seen if a person were to open their eyes. Those that are protected are canonized in the eyes of movies, television shows, so-called news articles, and the government. These protected classes can be seen by their place in society, and as they are portrayed. Additionally, such classes offer a service to the state, and the oligarchy that runs it. While some groups that are integral parts to the system can be ridiculed, there are certain classes that are protected above all else. The protected identity of these groups is of utmost importance. So, if the narrative around any of these groups was impacted, this could bring about the destruction of the whole system.

The teachers in the school system is among the important classes of the propaganda system; possibly even the most important. Teachers can do no harm, and should never, ever, be questioned. They are the foundation to this system, as they indoctrinate the people from an early age. While the minds of people are still forming, it is important to mold them into malleable peasant slaves, and keep them from experiencing alternatives. It is the experience, along with emotions, that solidify a memory and the perspective of a human being. Therefore, the idea of the school teacher, protecting the minds of those most fragile, must never be tarnished. While many despise their high school teachers, upon elevation to college the damage is done, and Stockholm syndrome sets in. The University boosts the ego of each individual, who has been molded into a perfect agent of the system, and, after some time, they will forget all the atrocities that were committed against them in previous schools, and will subjected their children to the same treatment. With the promise of a brighter future, the perfectly molded individual will forget detention, harassment for not fitting in, and how the teacher never took their side. They were always a delinquent, while the teacher's favorites were always perfect little examples of the Hitler youth stereotype; spreading rumors and enforcing peer pressure. In fact, some of the memories, like detention, will become proud moments in their adult lives. While their perspectives were becoming shaped, their first kiss, and other moments that took place, will become hallmarks of their lives. While their own children suffer through the molding process, the parents will relive their fantasy childhood, through the pain of their own offspring. This is why it is almost considered a crime not to pay the teacher's wage, because they are poorly compensated public servants. Additionally, the teacher cannot be arrested, because they are cornerstones to society. In fact, yes, they are cornerstones to society, at least, for the one that is controlled by megalomaniac oligarchs.

The doctors & nurses can be compared to the teachers in importance, but they are not the true foundation to the system. While the doctors and nurses monitor the physical aspects of the peasants, they sometimes will work hand in hand with the teacher, and monitor the work that has been laid down. Should a person's mind rebel against their molding, psychologists and psychiatrists will set that individual back on their right path. Furthermore, while the protected position of the psychiatrist and psychologist took many, many, decades to solidify, they depend on the protection afforded to nurses, doctors, and teachers. The mind doctors can be seen as an insulated member of the protected classes, like the inner layers of an onion. Meanwhile, as anyone who has actually attempted to prosecute a malpractice suit would know, the defenders of our societal cornerstones will come out of the woodwork. Letters will begin arriving, speaking about the great sacrifices nurses and doctors make. In fact, the protected nature of the medical class can be seen in the propagandists' message that they are essential workers. If there are no more nurses or doctors, then people will die, and the whole world will stop spinning. However, if we examine what the doctor and nurse actual offer, in reality, we can see their importance. The drugs that a doctor prescribes damages the mind and body, just enough, to keep a person from rebelling against their molding. Additionally, the nurse will monitor and enforce the orders of the doctor, ensure they have absolute control over the health of their subjects. As the teacher refers to its subject as a student, the doctor refers to its patient. However, these two words can be replaced by subject, with little trouble.

The priests are guardians of the soul, and, despite frequent crimes of those most abhorrent nature, the priest retains trust in the public. This is because the priest, whether catholic or Muslim, is the voice of the creator. In reality, these agents are voices of the propaganda machine, and guard the emotions of their molded subjects. They use many tactics to solidify control over the emotions, which they refer to as the soul; despite this having nothing to do with an actual soul. One of the main tactics is the use of speech with music, which will lull their subjects into a malleable form. A favorite among cult leaders, it will be followed by a rigorous and emotionally engaging speech, which is then followed by more music and a calming tone. This process can differ slightly, depending on the particular religion, but the outcome is always the same. People are taught that they must depend on the church, mosque, temple, or synagogue. If the individual were to stray out on their own, they would lose the protection of their herd, but the system would also lose control of their molded subject. Therefore, it matters not what scandal the priest is involved in, because their zealous subjects will punish any dissenter with righteous justice. The reason that people will react so strongly, and often violently, when the image of the priest is challenged, is because this system specifically controls the emotions. Therefore, it can be very dangerous to challenge the image. Now, on this subject, it is important to notice the obvious break away from the Christian religion, by the propaganda system. The formation of independent churches, and so-called religious cults, destroyed much of the control that the system retained over Christianity; especially with an emphasis on a self-sought faith. While the banking oligarchs still retain a great foothold in the religion, they have begun a desperate transfer towards their new religion, or the much easier to manipulate Muslim religion. The new religion is that of the New Age Identity, and its followers can be seen through their rhetoric and uniform style, which pretends to stand out by fitting in.

Blue hair, boys that look like girls, and girls that look like boys, are hallmarks of this religion. However, when it comes to Islam, this lifestyle is abhorred. So, how do the religions of Islam and the New Identity mesh. That can be simply answered with another question. How do Muslims trust the system that constantly refers to them as terrorists? The religion of Islam is well established, similar to Christianity, to control the emotions of their molded subjects. This concept can be applied equally to Buddhism, Hinduism, and any religion that teaches dependence on a centralized structure, because that structure is controlled by banking clans and those that call themselves the elite. Finally, while other vocations are important to the system, and can be classified under a protected class, these three are the most important. They are the cornerstones of subject control, and the society that is controlled by a central bank, which does the bidding of a few old families. As a last note, those that enforce the control are easily seen, and it is through a top down system. A principal will come along, and tell everyone what to do, followed by the voice of reason, which says go along to get along. Then, the obvious puppet, will say that no mention should be made to the children, and any disagreement must be voiced behind closed doors, in order to maintain a "united front" against the children; as they will seek to exploit any weakness among the so-called adults. Naturally, when thought about logically, this is the height of childish behavior, which is a direct representation of the oligarchs that inherited these systems of control.

Masters of Matter

While the system, and banking oligarchs, seek to take everything of importance, the seizure of production is a necessary tenant; in their constant efforts to expand control. They must control everything that is produced, water, food, air, and trees: everything. This process came about through many methods, but once the production of all things has taken hold, they have absolute and complete control. It matters little who sells the products, or for how much, if a person can control the production. In fact, when it comes to the so-called robber barons of the Americas, the game of production seizure, and using one's position to dominate the world, becomes increasingly more apparent. The banking clans seized the very production of wealth. Taking the example of a hedge fund manager, or investor, the banking clans produce trade and commerce. Therefore, anyone that becomes an opponent to them, can easily be thrown out of society; although, opponents are usually just eliminated. One of the most important products for these people to seize, in order to solidify control, is the production of firearms. When it comes to the old black powder firearm, regulation and production was very difficult to manage. An individual person could build their own musket, while a rifle would be harder to obtain. This is because basic blacksmithing skills could be applied to build the firearm. While many argue that firearms are just as easy, if not easier, for the average person to build, it is not the production of firearms that was ultimately seized. Instead, the core component to the firearm, the projectile, is dominated and controlled by a few state protected monopolies. While in olden days, a regular person could make a batch of black powder, as the components are relatively easy to acquire even today, the primer for modern cartridges, and smokeless powder, are extremely difficult to form. There might be a revolution in ammunition production in the future, but, currently, a trusted few dominate and control the production of these components. The reason for this control is simple, the compounds are simply too dangerous to be synthesized by an ordinary person. It is certainly a dangerous venture to defy the state, and attempt synthesis of one's own primer and powder compound. Sure, powder and primers can be bought over the counter, but their production is controlled. It is under the governance of a few, who only bide their time for the right moment to shut down sale to the masses. This will not take place until strike anywhere matches, and other components of homemade compounds, have also been removed from the public sphere. Once this is accomplished, all the oligarchs have to do is stop sale of primers and compounds to the public, allowing access only to their own enforcement agents.

Continuing on this theme, the seizing of the language is incredibly important. This can be accomplished through a myriad of ways, but the most common includes control over the dictionaries, and the over use of a single word. Coordinated through all of their channels, a shift in the function and use of a word takes place; thus, a new meaning for one word will become arbitrarily changed. Furthermore, while the position of linguists can be problematic, the seizing and changing of language is a numbers game, and there are relatively few true linguists in the populace at large. It is simple, once the definition of the word has been changed in all the online dictionaries, the old definition will not be used, as that edition will be out-of-date. Thus, the new definition will then be solidified, as so-called news articles, movies, television shows, and politicians will all simultaneously use this word in the new context. Now, a person would imagine this taking place naturally, and solely the product of a popular fad. However, nothing could be further from the truth, and the example of the word Google is applicable. The word Google suddenly, seemingly overnight, became a staple of not only the English language, but also Spanish, Portuguese, and others. This took place in a myriad of ways. First, the mockingbird media and Hollywood worked together to solidify the term, such as a character on Buffy the Vampire slayer using the word Google as a verb, in a sentence, and then explaining what the word signified. Like so many child shows, teaching a word through examples and repetition, the word Google became a staple in the English language. Furthermore, to win any argument, all a person has to do is Google the answer, and anything else is false, because it is not on Google. Through a short period of time, one company, ruled and run by a secretive state entity, became the arbiter and controller of truth and language. The online dictionaries that change the meaning of words are pushed to the top of a google search, along with examples of use in context, following the pattern of our molding in the indoctrination system of schools.

Now, seizure of the production of nature was a bit more difficult, and theoretically impossible. However, this did not stop the power mongers from doing their best to bring nature under their dominion. Cloud seeding is a prime example of seizing the production of natural forces. Cloud seeding, as the name suggests, takes place by artificially forming clouds, possibly through ionizing the atmosphere, and, subsequently, seizing the production of rain. This can be helpful in changing seasons, and water crops in regions that normally do not receive rain. However, because nature depends on balance, attempting to seize the production of natural forces can have dire and unpredictable consequences. When one region receives rain, outside of its own cycle, this will mean another region of the world will receive a, un-characteristic, drought. Furthermore, this is not the only example of seizing the production of nature. In fact, many methods have been used to dominate and control people, or divert resources to more worthy subjects. As an example, Saddam Hussein is reported to have diverted water away from the Iraqi wetlands; thus, draining them, and greatly harming the rebellious people that resided there. Now, as these attempts to control nature can have drastic consequences, an explanation for uncommon shifts in weather patterns and natural environments had to be invented. So, the so-called concept of environmentalism was born.

Now, if these people can seize the production of weather, then seizing that of food and water should be relatively easy. This was mainly accomplished through the poisoning of water and food. Once the public distrusted the natural outlets, that would not be within the system's control, people would begin to rely on the outlets that the oligarch's control. The streams, rivers, and lakes were poisoned, but the most effective tool to move people away from natural water sources was fear. In fact, they even admit poising the water supplies, although they use the word contamination. Once a few people became sick, and with the reporting of some deaths, all people became afraid of the natural outlets for water. Therefore, the most effective tool here was fear. After all, sediment filters out harmful elements, and places necessary minerals in water. The same thing took place with food. Poisoning food, especially those made by unlicensed individuals, meant only FDA approved products would ever be purchased. With the tried and true method of poisoning the body and mind, production of these elements could be completely seized. However, they did not stop there. Since the production was under their control, these people even poisoned the food and water that they disseminate. Now, why would they do this? The simple answer, among others, is to slowly damage the bodies of their subjects. In this way, the masses would be less physically resilient, and less of a threat to their power. Of course, their enforcement mechanisms would be well taken care of. Meanwhile, obesity, and other food and water related problems, help these people retain control over their subjects in the world. Now, in order to explain the process of water poisoning, we shall look at late 19th and early 20th century London. While advancements in medicine and sanitation practices are often pointed to for the removal of cholera as a problem, this issue does not appear as a major issue in many parts of history, or the world. Of course, agents of the system would deny this fact. In fact, this was one of the best excuses, among others, to begin placing chlorine in drinking water. First of all, the brewers in London never got sick from cholera, because they drank beer all the time, but another element is very important to this example. Those that dig and drink from their own wells, or natural sources, almost never contract a water borne illness. Furthermore, most with half a brain know that running water, and sediment, filter out bad components. Additionally, a strong immune system can fight off any disease, bacteria, or other harmful substance. So, pressing on with the example, a rational person would lay the contamination of the public water systems at the feet of those who controlled it, but it is truly astounding that the logical solution was to add yet more poison to the water. The chemical known as chlorine is very destructive to the body, and can cause irreparable damage to brain function, as well as respiratory and heart problems. In fact, most of the health and sanitation departments enforce the poisoning of our food, mainly through pesticides, and our water, with chlorine, and they can make these horrid actions with impunity, because they do so for the purpose of establishing control over the masses.

Institutions

School, prison, & the military are all the same, and listed as the only choices for a future. There are few alternatives to these three choices, and any will be met with harsh persecution. Outside of these spheres, the state has no control, so these three choices are the ones offered. Those that choose an alternative will likely end up in prison, on some bogus charge, because the system cannot allow for dissenters, or anyone to escape its clutches. Compounds, convents, communes, or any other attempted alternative ideas will bring the full attention, and wrath, of the state. In fact, many hunters are arrested and imprisoned for poaching, because they forgot to update their license, or a new and bogus environmental law was passed. In fact, the state, controlled by an oligarchy of foreign bankers, attempts to force everyone into one of these three choices. Whether a person chooses school, prison, or the military, all three are structured the same, and meet the same fate. In some cases, a prisoner has more rights than a school student, or a member of the military. This is because, as the prisoner has no stated rights, they have no recourse, and so the state has complete dominance over them. Thus, they are given some leeway, as long as they understand it is at the privilege of the state, to which they are slaves. On the other hand, the members of the military were still covered under the problematic constitution, at least until the Uniform Code of Military Justice alleviated that particular nuisance. Now, the student also claims the Constitution as their birth right, which is still an issue that the system faces today. Many approaches have been taken, but the Department of Education was able to change the meanings of definitions, with the help of dictionary makers; subsequently, changing the meaning of the constitution. Whichever path that you choose, it will be no choice at all. You will only have the illusion of a future to contemplate, and all paths will be controlled by the state.

The Federal Aviation Administration, the Transportation Security Administration, the Customs and Border Protection, the Department of Transportation, the United States Citizenship and Immigration Services and other affiliated organizations, dominate and control all modes of human travel. Coordinating their efforts with other such institutions around the globe. They are a major part of the fascist cabal, which makes decisions that regular people cannot make. They also suppress any advancements in technology that would damage their control. In fact, it takes only a small amount of logic to understand what their purpose is. None of these organizations were formed by, nor for, the people. Instead, they are enforcers of the world order, that seeks to dominate and control all life. Take for instance the passport, most people do not think along these lines, but any animal without papers is an illegal occupant of the land, in which they reside. A dog or cat that is missing their shots can be treated as illegal, and if they have a so-called owner, the owner is held accountable for state mandated treatment. In order to travel, the animal must have a passport. In fact, these people desire control and domination over everything, even the migration of birds. They tag and track bird migrations, always saying that it is to track the migration patterns for research, which is only partially true. While the transportation of birds is one thing, the domination and suppression of human travel is similar to that of livestock. Certain livestock is not allowed to travel from one place to another, as they are regulated. The purpose to this regulation is often not what is reported. Additionally, those that travel for purposes other than tourism are treated like criminals, regardless of which country they come from. This is because the travel of humanity is regulated by the same individuals that regulate and control every other aspect of our lives, including birth, death, marriage, and all other parts that were once private. In fact, there has never been less freedom in history then the age in which we currently live. In the example of the United States, these agencies make it extremely difficult for foreigners to enter the country legally, and shockingly easy to enter illegally. This is because those that control these elements desire slaves, and illegal immigrants are much easier to control than citizens. They do not want more citizens, constantly claiming the Constitution and raising awareness for problematic freedom. Instead, an illegal immigrant can always be threatened with deportation, bodily harm, or even death, because immigrants have no rights, and the same applies to citizens of the United States that leave the country. Outside of the United States, a citizen has no rights, not even the right to demand services from their own governmental entities. This is because U. S. Citizens do not actually control the U. S. Government.

Moving on, the cellular network is controlled and enforced through the FCC, which stifles any and all innovation that challenges its authority. The cellular companies are nothing more than state protected monopolies, and possibly state run. They are no different than the 18th century trading monopolies, under the

European powers, which made any other traders into illegal smugglers. While the European trade monopolies were vastly unsuccessful, the Federal Communications Commission has managed to take control of every aspect of what we once regarded as open communication. Additionally, the only portion of communication technology that has a small modicum of freedom, the HAM radio networks, have come under heavy attack by the FCC, and its overlords, or allies. This organization is simply yet another that takes power from the people, and puts it back into the hands of the oligarchs of decades past. The FCC, and partner organizations, ensures we remain in the stone age, with bulky cell towers, and relatively slow internet and cellphone speeds. Naturally, any upgrade to these networks is either the opposite, or a repackaged version of the same thing. These organizations can track, record, and collect data on anyone, when they control the very physical highways of communication. They certainly don't want any innovation spoiling that control, and putting a cell tower in every house in America. Unlike older technology, a small device cannot act as a base station for cell phones. Additionally, as anyone who has signed up for internet knows, each major provider is assigned a territory, and the FCC protects this territory. Good luck attempting any start-up communication business, as it will be shut down almost immediately. This corrupt organization represents a peak of fascist ideology, and the antithesis to so-called capitalism, or rather free and fair trade.

2020

The staged riots of the year 2020 did the most to open the eyes of many. However, while they can only see a small piece of the puzzle, the overall picture board is still obscured. Despite horrid treatment by institutions they used to trust, the public at large still puts their faith in many of the same organizations. Unfortunately, it might take many decades to completely remove the absolute control that has been re-established over the past centuries. The good news lies in our positive trajectory. Due to their own actions, those that previously held, mostly uncontested, influence over the minds of the world are quickly losing what they had inherited. This is what can be called the inheritance syndrome, when the successors do not understand the lessons of their forefathers; arrogantly, believe they, themselves, are superior. Now, when it comes to the subject of riots, a few elements are extremely obvious. Unfortunately, due to a scrubbing of the internet archives, much of the evidence of these events has been purged. Still, there are alternative places to find this evidence, but much has been wiped clean. Instead, the firsthand account of live streams will be used, to explain this process. At the beginning of the riots, a large portion of the brainwashed population, especially college students, flocked to the cause. It really did seem like we were nearing the end, at first. That is because many of the first protesters truly believed they were doing good, despite being tricked. Now, one specific example shows how the staging occurred. First, during one of these riots in a northern state, trash trucks had been lined up to block an intersection. These trucks were then burned, and plastered over every propaganda outlet the next day. Furthermore, at the beginning of these riots, all of the propaganda outlets were running the same message over and over again, attempting to rally others to their cause. In formation, these riots used a protest as a cover, but this was less necessary when it came to the police. Clearly, the stagers of the riots were working in conjunction with local uniformed services, while ambushing and killing, or wounding, any uniformed dissenters. The cohesion between the rioting groups and the state services was apparent throughout the year. In fact, one group of alleged insurrectionists was surrounded by a strong force of locals, when the police came to their salvation. Furthermore, while the groups constantly preached aggression towards the police officer, in reality they struck hardest against local citizens and businesses. Working together, the police and the rioters came against the citizens, hoping to scare them into bowing before the state. Whenever it was time, the police would move the rioters in their assigned direction. Fortunately, the support for these groups dwindled over time, and the armed citizens' resistance that they faced took away all the protection of the state. Many realized that they state might guard their salaries, but a bullet could end their lives. While the propaganda machine continues to spread their fear mongering, the majority has turned their backs, and left behind the bogus mockingbird causes. Of course, as with all things, the state tested the protest beforehand, at Ferguson. This move was partially brilliant, as so many were focused on a physical virus, they did not understand that the virus was in the mind. The use of fear in chaos would drive more chaos, spreading like a virus. Everything that was implemented in the year 2020 was to spread a mental virus, claiming the world in a shower of fire and death; reducing a large portion of the global population in the process.

The armed citizens in 2020 is the only thing that saved the United States of America from total collapse, which cannot be said for other parts of the world. Instead of completely burning down the country, rioters were segregated to only certain parts; mainly major cities. Now, the major cities are almost in ruins, while the rest of the country saw very little destruction. The cause of this is two-fold. First, the citizens outside of the major cities refused to bow to curfews, lockdowns, and a manufactured shutdown of the economy; which completely devastated the major centers. In a comical turn of events, the propagandists' shutdown and burned their own strongholds; thinking they had more control then they actually did. The high population of armed citizens, outside of the city centers, only needed to gather, in a show of force, to scare away the agents of the state. This done, the majority went back to their private lives, as if nothing had taken place. Some small groups of armed citizens, usually paid, did protect some of the local businesses in the city centers, but most were left to their chosen fates. This is because few of the city folk requested aide. Instead, city center dwellers falsely believed that bowing before the state would save them. Fortunately, the state driven destruction was stopped by citizens, mostly outside of its control. The economy of the United States of America stayed strong, due to the efforts of the armed citizen, rather than those that believed that they are in absolute control.

Now, the pedophile phenomenon in the year 2020 possibly made the most impact on the oligarchical control structures. The exposure of pedophilia related to royal family members, Hollywood stars, and high ranking politicians made one of the greatest impacts against their control. While local sheriffs and the U. S. Marshal services conducted raids against child trafficking rings, many of which were protected by local police forces and federal agencies, the rest of the public focused on the big named individuals. The Epstein Did Not Kill Himself meme was wildfire on social media, invading every social media group and spoken on the lips of nearly every individual. While the meme was mostly a joke, the general reaction was complete disgust in our self-appointed leaders. The majority ceased to look further than the meme, but it still played in impact. Now, for those that dug further, the cesspool of evil actions seemed to have no end. The entire world, it seemed, was run by those with the most disturbing of fetishes. Much of what was reported about them, by alternative outlets, and backed by evidence, was beyond imagining. The idea of adrenochrome harvesting, taken from the adrenaline of a tortured child, was so abhorrent that many chose not to believe it. However, the scandals did not stop there. Nearly the entirety of Hollywood could be linked to child sex slavery, along with many CEOs, politicians, and a certain British prince. In fact, a furniture company was found to have smuggled children, inside of bookcases and such, which was essentially an online store for oligarchical pedophiles. While this particular rabbit hole goes very deep, as the curtain was drawn back, many simply could not continue to look. Rather, faces turned away, and people chose to label these events as conspiracy theories, despite evidence, because the implications would be too much to bear. Every single person on the planet bore responsibility, for allowing this evil to persist, and most could not handle that reality.

Adding to the rampant chaos of 2020, which was, in-reality, less chaotic then reported. Assassinations were very prevalent throughout the year. In fact, some assassinations were even reported on by the mockingbird media, although caution should always be taken when working with these deceptive outlets. A judge's son was shot by a delivery man, while others in connection were found dead in similar circumstances, on opposite sides of the continent. However, only the child of the judge was reported on, but it took only a little effort to find connected stories. Other assassinations were less obvious, and many were attributed to the alleged virus, or natural causes. While none had the desire to bring light to any of the assassinations, whether ordered by the cabal, or their adversaries, many appeared rather convenient for one side, or the other. A lot of what happened in the year 2020 is difficult to decipher, on the surface, and the multiple assassinations over the year are no different. In fact, many might even be considered executions. Such as the deaths of Ruth Bader Ginsberg, a particular favorite of the propaganda system, and a laundry list of celebrities. However, while Ginsberg's death became an overly beaten dead horse, many of the celebrities, that died in 2020, passed quietly.

Meanwhile, the meme war of 2020 is another aspect to the war against the cabal's control; including the Pepe Meme, Trash Dove, Boogaloo, Red Pill, and the song Fortunate Son, by Creedence Clearwater Revival. Now, each of these elements have their own importance, and many others could be added to the list. The Red Pill, a reference to the Matrix franchise, was a perfectly thought-out analogy for bringing people's attention to the reality of their situation. Being red-pilled was synonymous with waking up, also a reference to the Matrix, and understanding that freedom and individual liberty had been taken away; in the dead of night, through trickery and intrigue. The color of the pill also correlated with the political campaign of President, and real-estate mogul, Donald Trump, which was contrasted with the blue color of the opposition. Now, the blue pill, in the matrix franchise, erased memory and left the subject asleep, unaware of their fake reality. Furthermore, the red flag was raised to signify total war, in the past; when the color of flags was still important. This meant that no prisoners would be taken, and any enemy encountered would be destroyed. Total war is an "us or them" style of conflict. Now, the boogaloo, Pepe the frog, and trash dove memes kept the enemy of the red pill group distracted. The boogaloo distracted the Letter Agencies, that were constantly afraid of being turned into the infamous Alphabet Soup. Meanwhile, the Pepe army kept the rabid new age cult followers occupied, with constant harassment in the digital space. The Pepe army would post anything that the opposing side would find offensive. While the Pepe the frog meme revolved around Nazi symbolism, something that the drove the real Nazis mad, the boogaloo used old military references; which shows the main population of these groups. While both had constant infiltration by paid opposition, these infiltrators were always obvious. The agency infiltrators in the boogaloo movement would spread fear propaganda, and seek to trick members into self-implication. However, lacking creativity, these bureaucratic agents of the state were easy to spot. With the case of the Pepe meme, clearly the younger civilian generation of video gamers staffed their ranks, as most of their works were based around such references; conjoined with hacker style tactics. Meanwhile, the red pill sudo-movement, along with the Q-Anons, were populated by the older generations; which were focused on change through logic, analysis, and reason. Now, the trash dove meme had less of a role, especially when compared to the Pepe meme, but it was a staple element during the beginning. The trash dove was going to be used by the propaganda system to bring more child soldiers into the fold, but was tainted by the Pepe army. All of this took place in, what many have called, the information war, which included the meme war. While the information was fought across all communication methods, the meme war was, specifically, contested within the social media spheres. Our would-be oligarchical overlords believe they have won this war, because they control the highway of information, and censored any dissenters. However, after much of their user base was woken up, those that were censored simply moved to other places; which are not under oligarchical control. Therefore, the administrators of these highways simply lost control, essentially having opposing bypasses built around them. Now, these platforms are mostly a cesspool of hatred, including the few brainwashed people that are left. Although, at this point, any, that have not awoken, are asleep by choice.

Agenda 21 was an important element in the 2020 information war, which sometimes turned physical, and was the main strategy of the oligarchs. While it was laid out, in relatively plain language, during the 1992 summit, in Rio de Janeiro, Agenda 21 had a long period for implementation. Since their plans were easily discovered, and thwarted, these oligarchs felt the need to implement their strategy sooner. This meant they were panicked and shot their proverbial wad early on. The Agenda 21 was the strategy of these oligarchs to bring their final blow against the people; reducing the global population and solidify their control over those that were left, while removing any dissenters. The rational for this strategy was to protect the environment, a commonly used excuse for the expansion of state control. This was a warfare strategy, but, due to their arrogance, the oligarchs believed none would catch on, and they greatly underestimated the strength of their opposition. While the war continues, the soldiers of the oligarchs continue their attempts to implement this strategy, but they get weaker with each passing day. Masking and lockdowns were a part of this agenda, seeking to destroy the global economy, and sew chaos and disorder. The staged riots were also a part of this plan, all with the aim of mobilizing their followers, frightening those in the middle to submit, and removing the dissenters; which they believed were only a few. Dominion and Scytl were also elements in this plan, seeking to solidify absolute control over the voting processes, by bringing them within the internet domain; which they had absolute control over, through ICANN. Now, while certain individuals, like Rudy Giuliani and Sidney Powell championed awareness of the internet voting strategy, Project Veritas, led by James O'Keef, approached this portion of the agenda from another angle. The deck had been stacked for a long time, presenting a fantasy of choice to us for generations, as voting fraud schemes had been prevalent for a long time. Project Veritas uncovered multiple ballot harvesting schemes, and people that would falsify their identity, some even voting multiple times. However, the most insidious of all the schemes uncovered pertained to the immigrant populations in Minnesota. One of the darkest tactics was used in this area to elect a member of another nation's royalty to the United States' Congress, named Ilhan Omar. While massive ballot harvesting and fraud was taking place here, the residents, of Somali origin, were being threatened, possibly even with a gun to their heads, to submit fraudulent votes for her. While this is likely not an isolated incident, Project Veritas's coverage certainly increased an understanding of the operations involved; to establish Agenda 21.

Words of the Wise

The nomad slaves, that rose up and steam rolled over their arrogant overlords, taught us one method for dealing with evil tyranny. Timujin, himself being a slave, declared total war on the royal houses that oppressed nomads, and any that stood with them. There would be no trials, there would be no quarter, and all royalty they encountered were destroyed. In fact, one prince, who ruled over a region that incorporated modern day Iran, was the only to escape the nomad wrath; fleeing to the Indian subcontinent, where influence of the nomad slave network ended. While this no quarter method against tyrants worked, establishing an unforeseen peace across the once volatile region, the Mongols eventually became what they had sought to destroy. Proving a far reaching, corrupting, influence and temptation to control. In fact, the Venetian guilds had much to do with the corruption of Mongols, but it was they, the Mongols, that chose to forget.

Moving on, the Revolutionary Smugglers, establishing constitutions, and attempting to secure freedom for all, did a great job of combating the world wide tyranny. As with the Mongols, the majority of the heroes were forgotten, replaced with the names of plants, and other figures, all with the purpose of shifting the narrative. The founding fathers, and other top down figures, are credited with building the nation, the genius of drafting the documents that limited their own power. However, this makes little sense, as does the magical writings of Voltaire, Paine, and others. This tactic can be seen used over and over again, with the shifting of narratives, and manipulation of history. However, with a little logic, one can discover the nonsensical nature of the narrative. With the Alcohol Tobacco and Firearms Agency, or ATF, they credit their history to a rebellion that took place in 1790, which is no great event in history, but it shows the true nature and purpose of the agency. What could easily be called a Farmers Rebellion, was more of an armed protest, with no real fighting. This happened when congress sought to expand its control, and ignore the very articles they had signed, by passing a tax on distilled spirits; if this event was real in the first place, and not a fiction. Now, the ATF, and state endorsed historians, would have you believe that this was over whiskey, calling it the Whiskey Rebellion, and that farmers consumed it. However, the congress of the time wished to tax something made for preservation, and harvested during wheat processing. This was akin to the window and soap taxes from England. It was unenforceable, and was soon repealed, but the damage was done. Therefore, to imagine that this congress, that attempting to impose tyranny on the people, immediately after signing a document that curbed their power, were the true inventors of such a document is illogical in the highest order. While there is a lot to unravel, as much has been obfuscated, the influence of the American Indian can give insight into the countries true origins, along with the influence of the Prussian and the American smuggler. Rhode Island, and their lucrative, and illicit, rum trade would be another good starting point. Either way, many of the founding fathers are likely bogus, along with other figures of the enlightenment period. To blindly follow these reported figures, and leaved such events unquestioned, for the sake of emotional attachment, will mean all of those true heroes died in vain; the ones that will never be mentioned in state sanctioned propaganda, with some even still banned. One such author, whose works are still being censored, is Jonathan Swift. A writer from earlier periods, he wrote Gulliver's Travels, which as book that is abhorred by the state's indoctrination department; the Department of Education, or, at least, it is presented to be so. Also, he wrote a Modest Proposal, which perfectly lays out the same child trafficking rings that are being uncovered today, and the evil that happens within; written a satire, of course.

Meanwhile, the sheriffs, the only constitutionally recognized peace keeping force on the continent, also provides insight into our true origins. Since the sheriffs are elected by the people, they are abhorred by the global oligarchs. Therefore, anything the oligarchs hate must be examined carefully, for they only hate that which challenges their control. The unconstitutional police forces are run by officials that are elected by an oligarchy, a city council, and funded by the banking oligarchs, but the sheriff is a completely different system. Despite their best efforts, the sheriffs could not be completely destroyed, but their budgets could be reduced, along with their jurisdiction. Without the will or consent of the people, the global banking oligarchs were able to completely neuter our sheriffs, elected to protect the people, while installing their own enforcement officers, charged with establishing tyranny over the people. One of the few paths back to the intention of the founding, structured by the people, and not an oligarchy of saviors, is through the sheriffs. While it might be a pipe dream, the agencies, police forces, highway patrol agencies, and every other state control mechanism, must be removed; with their funding going back to the sheriffs, to whom peace keeping taxes were originally paid. Furthermore, when posing this idea, expected ridicule, and state sanctioned crackdown, is almost a guarantee, because they despise having their control challenged, because none of these mechanisms exist by or for the people, they are enemies of the people. Only the sheriffs, elected by the people, have constitutional authority to operate as they do; all others are illegal occupying forces. Furthermore, as nearly every federal outlet, especially the military, are staffed by state citizens, the states ultimately retain power to reign in the federal government. Not only could the states recall their members in the military, they could also remove federal agents from their territories. In fact, the federal government is in a precarious position, depending on the discretion of the states, and they fear state legislatures realizing the power that each truly possesses.

Now, cross-Referencing is a path to understanding, and will allow for a better picture; when researching through the manipulated and obfuscated annals of history. With cross referencing, multiple propaganda outlets can be compared, and truth devised from the between the lies. Where multiple propaganda outlets meet, as long as they are truly separate, truth can be found. An example of this can be seen with the Osage Empire, when ministers of the Spanish Empire wrote to their king about a war taking place. This was entirely fabricated, and referred to as the Osage-Spanish paper war, because it took place only on paper. Afraid of being beheaded for their inability to subjugate the rebellious Osage, the Spanish ministers chose to pretend. Furthermore, they could not declare war on the Osage, as they Osage would take up the call; and Osage recourse would be swift and total. Now, were there only documentation by the Spanish, this event would have been reported as a fact in state run propaganda curriculums. However, because the French, English, and United States governments covered this period also, in the same region, and contradicted the reports of the Spanish, it can be confirmed that no actual war took place. Naturally, any documentation that the Osage would have kept would be destroyed, as that would contradict the narrative of the illiterate savage. However, records are kept in the beadwork and tapestries, but the ability to read them may have been lost over the ages. Furthermore, the Osage are mainly ignored by the indoctrination outlets, specifically because of the ability to cross-reference. First and foremost, the cross-referencing of firsthand accounts is the best way to discover truth, but simple firsthand accounts are not enough. Going straight to the horse's mouth is preferred. Even if the horse's mouth is stuffed with excrement, it will still give a great amount of insight into the source. Finally, prizing ability over accolade, sometimes referred to as a meritocracy, is very important to finding our way back. Merit means skill and ability, but it also includes creativity. Those that rely on accolade, will always, eventually, succumb to those with talent, ability, and creativity, because those that depend on surface achievements, and self-aggrandizement, will always lose to someone with ability. Since these oligarchs abhor any that can outshine them, they will ultimately fall to those that they have vilified, because they cannot purchase that which they do not themselves possess. The truly talented and skilled are not found in expensive toilet paper, also called degrees, nor in multiple choice tests, but they are forged in practice, and found in the same. This is why the state run indoctrination and propaganda outlets try so hard to taint practice and ability, saying only con artists demean the importance of degrees and accolades, but this is divorced from reality. They will go down screaming about how their demise is impossible, while those that they have enslaved wash over them like a flood, as the Mongols did, as the smugglers of the eighteenth century did, and as we will do once more. Now, some tactics have been shown to be successful, the distraction and time wasting efforts of the Pepe and Boogaloo kept agents running down dead ends. President Donald Trump used a classic cult breaking tactic, in upstaging the leaders. Regardless of whatever tactic is chosen, it is important to take one lesson from the oligarchs. Always choose the most effective strategy, and, in one move, hit multiple birds with one stone.

Books by This Author

The Rainbow Reich

www.ingramcontent.com/pod-product-compliance
Lightning Source LLC
Chambersburg PA
CBHW070957250726
48663CB00002B/263